English

Assessment Papers
Up to Speed

10–11+ years

Great Clarendon Street, Oxford, OX2 6DP, United Kingdom

Oxford University Press is a department of the University of Oxford. It furthers the University's objective of excellence in research, scholarship, and education by publishing worldwide. Oxford is a registered trade mark of Oxford University Press in the UK and in certain other countries

Text © Sarah Lindsay 2015
Illustrations © Oxford University Press 2015

The moral rights of the authors have been asserted

First published in 2015
This edition published in 2022

All rights reserved. No part of this publication may be reproduced, stored in a retrieval system, or transmitted, in any form or by any means, without the prior permission in writing of Oxford University Press, or as expressly permitted by law, by licence or under terms agreed with the appropriate reprographics rights organization. Enquiries concerning reproduction outside the scope of the above should be sent to the Rights Department, Oxford University Press, at the address above.

You must not circulate this work in any other form and you must impose this same condition on any acquirer

British Library Cataloguing in Publication Data
Data available

978-0-19-278503-9

10 9 8 7 6 5 4 3

Paper used in the production of this book is a natural, recyclable product made from wood grown in sustainable forests.
The manufacturing process conforms to the environmental regulations of the country of origin.

Printed in Great Britain by Ashford Colour Ltd.

Acknowledgements

The publishers would like to thank the following for permissions to use copyright material:

Page make-up: OKS Prepress, India
Cover illustrations: Lo Cole

P12 'Aliens Stole My Underpants' by Brian Moses from *Behind the Staffroom Door: The Very Best of Brian Moses*, published by Macmillan (2007); p22 'The Great Mouse Plot' by Roald Dahl from *Boy – Tales of Childhood*, published by Jonathan Cape, an imprint of Penguin Books Ltd; p32 from *Victory* by Susan Cooper, published by Corgi Books (2007). Reproduced by permission of Random House Children's Books; p39 'The Apple Raid' by Vernon Scannell from *The Apple Raid*, published by Chatto & Windus (1974). Reproduced by kind permission of the author's estate; pp44–45 from *Stuff that scares your pants off!* by Glen Murphy, published by Macmillan Children's Books (2009); p50 'One Spared to the Sea' from *The Hogboon of Hell* by Nancy and W. Towrie Cutt, published by Andre Deutsch (1979).

Although we have made every effort to trace and contact all copyright holders before publication this has not been possible in all cases. If notified, the publisher will rectify any errors or omissions at the earliest opportunity.

Links to third party websites are provided by Oxford in good faith and for information only. Oxford disclaims any responsibility for the materials contained in any third party website referenced in this work

The manufacturer's authorised representative in the EU for product safety is Oxford University Press España S.A. of El Parque Empresarial San Fernando de Henares, Avenida de Castilla, 2 – 28830 Madrid (www.oup.es/en or product.safety@oup.com). OUP España S.A. also acts as importer into Spain of products made by the manufacturer.

Introduction

What is Bond?

The Bond *Up to Speed* titles are part of the Bond range of assessment papers, the number one series for the 11+, selective exams and general practice. Bond *Up to Speed* is carefully designed to support children who need less challenging activities than those in the regular age-appropriate Bond papers, in order to build up and improve their techniques and confidence.

How does this book work?

The book contains two distinct sets of papers, along with full answers and a Progress Chart:

- Focus tests, accompanied by advice and directions, are focused on particular (and age-appropriate) English question types encountered in the 11+ and other exams. The questions are deliberately set at a less challenging level than the standard *Assessment Papers*. Each Focus test is designed to help a child 'catch' their level in a particular question type, and then gently raise it through the course of the test and the subsequent Mixed papers.

- Mixed papers are longer tests containing a full range of English question types. These are designed to provide rigorous practice with less-challenging questions, perhaps against the clock, in order to help children acquire and develop the necessary skills and techniques for 11+ success.

Full answers are provided for both types of test in the middle of the book.

How much time should the tests take?

The tests are for practice and to reinforce learning, and you may wish to test exam techniques and working to a set time limit. Using the Mixed papers, we would recommend that your child spends 50 minutes answering the 80 questions in each paper, plus 5 minutes for reading the comprehension extract.

You can reduce the suggested time by 5 minutes to practise working at speed.

Using the Progress Chart

The Progress Chart can be used to track Focus test and Mixed paper results over time to monitor how well your child is doing and identify any repeated problems in tackling the different question types.

Focus test 1 — Spelling 1

Add the missing double letters to each of these words.

It is always important to recognise words that use double letters.

1. a _____ _____ ached
2. co _____ _____ ittee
3. a _____ _____ ompany
4. reco _____ _____ end
5. progra _____ _____ e
6. co _____ _____ espond

Each of these words has a silent letter. Circle the silent letter in each word.

Say the word out loud to help you hear which letter is silent.

7. island
8. knight
9. scenery
10. design
11. crumb
12. budget

Write the **plural** form of each of these **nouns**.

Remember, for most words ending in a consonant and y, you drop the y and add ies.

13. lady _____
14. country _____
15. toy _____
16. baby _____
17. trolley _____
18. fly _____

> If the root word takes the suffix 'tion' in its noun form, use the suffix 'tious'.

Add *cious* or *tious* to complete these words.

19 suspi_____
20 nutri_____
21 mali_____
22 vi_____
23 ficti_____
24 ambi_____

Add a **prefix** to each of these words to make a new word.

> A prefix is added to the beginning of a word to change its meaning.

un   im   il

25 _____broken
26 _____polite
27 _____pure
28 _____legal
29 _____founded
30 _____logical

Focus test 2 — Sentences 1

What are the following: commands, questions or statements?

Clue: what end punctuation mark would you use?

1. Shall we call at Georgia's house   _____
2. Why do I have to go to bed early   _____
3. Don't run   _____
4. It is nearly time for tea   _____
5. My ear is really sore   _____
6. Stop arguing with your brother   _____

Underline the letters in this passage that should be capitals.

Capital letters are used at the beginning of sentences and for proper nouns.

7–13   as emily ran towards cirencester park, she knew she was late. she just hoped archie had waited for her. he was going to swap his movie with her *harry potter* book but she knew he would be in a hurry.

Improve each of these sentences by adding a **clause** or **phrase**.

A clause is a section of a sentence with a main verb. A phrase is a group of words that act as a unit but do not include a main verb.

14   Mr Churchill kept an eye on the children in the pool.

_____

_____

15   The ponies roamed free on the moor.

_____

_____

16 The lioness showed her cubs the food.

_____

17 The car made a quick getaway.

_____

18 Jess watched a film.

_____

Change the word in bold into the **past tense**.

> If something is written in the past tense, it means it has already happened.

19 George **sleeps** in front of the television.   _____
20 Jacob **finds** his homework tricky.   _____
21 Aimee **rides** every week until the holiday.   _____
22 On Monday Aaron **goes** to judo.   _____
23 The dishwasher **makes** a funny sound.   _____
24 The rain **pours** throughout the night.   _____

Punctuate this sentence correctly.

> Don't forget (speech marks), commas, full stops and so on.

25–30 When will tea be ready moaned Freddie I'm starving It has to be soon

_____

_____

Now go to the Progress Chart to record your score!   Total   30

Focus test 3 — Grammar 1

Write two examples of each of the following.

> Proper noun – a naming word for a specific person, place or thing, beginning with a capital letter
>
> Abstract noun – a word referring to something that can't be identified with any of your five senses, such as an emotion or an idea
>
> Collective noun – a word referring to a group

1–2 proper noun _____ _____

3–4 abstract noun _____ _____

5–6 collective noun _____ _____

Form **verbs** from each of the following.

> These words are nouns, for example: the noun *production* gives the verb *produce*.

7 discussion _____

8 division _____

9 alteration _____

10 dictation _____

11 creation _____

12 celebration _____

Write an **adjectival phrase** about each of these **nouns**.

> An adjectival phrase gives more detail about a noun. It is comprised mostly of adjectives and does not include a main verb.

13 _____ pond

14 _____ cloud

15 _____ throne

16 _____ woman

17 _____ bone

18 _____ sportsman

Add a different **conjunction** to each of these sentences.

> Conjunctions are sometimes referred to as connectives. They are words that join together words, phrases or clauses.

19 The dog raced towards the pond _____ he got covered in mud!

20 Dan phoned Harry _____ he needed to ask him something.

21 The neighbours were irritating _____ they played their music too loud.

22 Ben finished his homework carefully _____ he could go out to play.

23 Megan ate her tea quickly _____ it gave her hiccups.

24 Jake laughed _____ he hadn't understood the joke.

Underline the **preposition** in each sentence.

> A preposition shows the position of one noun or noun phrase in relation to another.

25 The squirrel jumped towards the branch.

26 Hannah found her homework in the dog bed!

27 The mouse hid behind the pot plant.

28 Ben put his drink inside his bag.

29 I climbed over the fallen tree.

30 The pigeon sat alone on the telephone wire.

Now go to the Progress Chart to record your score!   Total   30

Focus test 4 — Vocabulary 1

Write an **abbreviation** for each of these.

An abbreviation is a word or words that are shortened.

1 Doctor   _____
2 United States   _____
3 centimetre   _____
4 Limited   _____
5 hour   _____
6 Great Britain   _____

Put these words in **alphabetical order**.

Alphabetical order is the order you would find words in a dictionary.

nun   nuzzle   nutmeg   number   nurse   nutty

7 _____   8 _____
9 _____   10 _____
11 _____   12 _____

Write a **metaphor** for each of these subjects.

A metaphor is an expression in which something is described in terms usually associated with something else, for example: 'the blanket of snow lay on the ground'.

13 a thick frost

_____

14 a duvet

_____

15 thunder

_____

16 a burning fire

_____

17 autumn leaves

_____

Underline the **root words** in each of these words.

> A root word is the word to which prefixes and suffixes are added to make another word.

18 unclean

19 agreeable

20 destructive

21 impure

22 inspection

23 planning

Using a word from each column, write seven **compound words**.

> A compound word is a word made up of two words, for example toothbrush.

24	night	dog
25	arm	due
26	bull	gown
27	chop	hole
28	day	chair
29	key	stick
30	over	dream

Focus test 5 — Comprehension 1

Aliens Stole My Underpants

To understand the ways
of alien beings is hard,
and I've never worked it out
why they landed in my backyard.

And I've always wondered why
on their journey to the stars,
these aliens stole my underpants
and took them back to Mars.

They came on a Monday night
when the weekend wash had been done,
pegged out on the line
to be dried by the morning sun.

Mrs Driver from next door
was a witness at the scene
when aliens snatched my underpants –
I'm glad that they were clean!

It seems they were quite choosy
as nothing else was taken.
Do aliens wear underpants
or were they just mistaken?

I think I have a theory
as to what they wanted them for,
they needed to block off a draught
blowing in through the spacecraft door.

Or maybe some Mars museum
wanted items brought back from space.
Just think of my pair of Y-fronts
displayed in their own glass case.

And on the label beneath
would be written where they got 'em
and how such funny underwear
once covered an Earthling's bottom!

Brian Moses

Answer these questions.

1. Where did the aliens land?

   _____

2. Where were the aliens believed to be heading?

   _____

3. Which day of the week did the aliens arrive?

   _____

4. Where did the aliens come from?

   _____

5–6. Write two pieces of evidence that suggest the aliens removed the underpants.

   _____

   _____

7. What is meant by line 17 'It seems they were quite choosy'?

   _____

8–9. What two reasons are given for the aliens' actions?

   _____

   _____

10. How do we know that this poem is written from a boy's perspective?

   _____

11. What is an 'Earthling' (line 32)?

   _____

12–13. Is this a rhyming poem? Give a reason for your answer.

   _____

   _____

14–15. Which verse do you most enjoy? Why?

   _____

   _____

   _____

Now go to the Progress Chart to record your score!   Total ( ) 15

Focus test 6 — Spelling 2

Circle the word that is spelled correctly.

These are tricky words. You may need a dictionary to help!

1. necessary — necessery
2. embarassed — embarrassed
3. sufficient — sufficiant
4. temprature — temperature
5. dictionary — dictionery
6. oppertunity — opportunity

Add *ance* or *ence* to each of these to make a word.

7. refer_____
8. obedi_____
9. extravag_____
10. lic_____
11. ignor_____
12. fragr_____

Circle the unstressed vowel in each of these words.

An unstressed vowel is a vowel within a word that is hard to hear.

13. general
14. secretary
15. interest
16. dictionary
17. original
18. family

Add *ie* or *ei* to each of these to make a word.

19 rev ___ ___ w   20 v ___ ___ l
21 th ___ ___ r   22 f ___ ___ rce
23 f ___ ___ ry   24 c ___ ___ ling

Write the **contraction** for each of these pairs of words.

> A contraction is when two words are shortened into one.

25 they + will   = _____
26 I + have   = _____
27 he + will   = _____
28 is + not   = _____
29 should + have   = _____
30 there + is   = _____

Focus test 7 — Sentences 2

Add the missing commas to these sentences.

> Commas are needed to separate clauses, phrases or items in a list. They can also be used for parenthesis, around a piece of information that adds information but is not vital for the sentence to make sense.

1. To make ice cubes pour cold water into the mould and put in the freezer.
2–3. The old lady frail and unsteady carried her shopping home.
4. Carys collected her certificate medal and winning prize money from the major.
5–6. The mango sweet and juicy tasted delicious.

Add the missing colons to these sentences.

> A colon can be used to introduce a list of items.

7. Kirkwood Secondary School specialises in two areas sport and technology.
8. Our journey took us on many modes of transport car, plane and train.
9. Aimee entered two classes in the local horse show the jumping class and the fancy-dress class.
10. I want you to bring the following things to school tomorrow a towel, your swimming costume and a change of clothes.
11. Tia loves many sports netball, swimming, football and tennis.

Draw a line (/) every time a new line should have started in the following dialogue.

> A new line should be started every time a new person starts to speak.

12–17 "I can't wait for the performance," said Ellie. "Nor can I!" replied Dan. "Which scene are you in?" asked Tuhil. "I'm in the first scene," said Dan. "I bet I feel very nervous the first time we do it." "I know I will be terrified but I still can't wait," laughed Izzy. "Shall we practise at playtime?" Ellie asked. "Great idea!" they all responded.

Rewrite these sentences, adding the missing punctuation and capital letters.

> Always check through your work carefully to make sure that you have picked up all the missing punctuation and capital letters.

18–22 please can i take your dog for a walk asked julia

23–30 i am so tired said simon yawning i am going to bed early tonight

Focus test 8 — Grammar 2

Write three sentences, each including an **adjective** and a **modal verb**.

> An adjective describes someone or something. A modal verb is a verb that changes the meaning of other verbs in a sentence, for example to say what <u>should</u> or <u>may</u> happen.

1–2 _____

3–4 _____

5–6 _____

Circle the **pronouns**.

> A pronoun is a word usually used to replace a noun.

7–12   up   mine   his   soon

       under   you   they   because

       theirs   know   see   I

Choose the **adverb** that would best describe each **verb**.

> An adverb provides information about place (for example, here), time (for example, soon), manner (for example, quickly) or the degree of possibility (for example, surely).

often   carefully   perhaps

soon   speedily   playfully

13   The sprinter ran _____.

14   I'm sure your grandparents will _____ arrive.

15   The cat _____ moved towards the mouse.

16   As the children _____ splashed in the pool, their mother looked on.

17   _____ it will be fish and chips for tea.

18   Molly _____ sat and read.

In each of these sentences a word is incorrect. Underline the word and rewrite it correctly.

Look carefully at the verbs!

19 The twins tried to caught the ball. _____

20 We think you would liked to go. _____

21 It were time to leave. _____

22 Jay had to ate his breakfast quickly. _____

23 Freya write a letter to her penfriend. _____

24 Elliot find a Roman coin. _____

Circle the word that is:

25	a verb	him	cake	going	up
26	an adjective	cloudy	jump	from	it
27	an adverb	leotard	there	was	party
28	a noun	several	his	choir	near
29	a preposition	shaded	love	me	beneath
30	a verb	now	ate	happily	onto

Focus test 9 — Vocabulary 2

Write six **synonyms** for the word 'see'.

> A synonym is a word with the same or similar meaning to another word.

1–6 _____ _____ _____

_____ _____ _____

Write two **onomatopoeic** words that describe the sound this thing makes.

> Onomatopoeic words echo a sound associated with its meaning.

7–8 a cat   _____   _____

9–10 a car   _____   _____

Match, with a line, the **formal** words with the **informal** options.

> It is important to recognise the difference between formal and informal words so you can choose the appropriate style to use in different situations.

11 commence   end
12 request   try
13 terminate   ask for
14 endeavour   start

Write a **definition** for each of these words.

> A definition is the meaning of a word.
> Use a dictionary to help if you are stuck on a word.

15 invisible

_____

16 drowsy

_____

17 soundproof

_____

18 verdict

_____

Circle the **diminutives**.

> A diminutive is a word implying smallness.

19–24
goose	droplet	minibus	flute
kitchenette	fly	piglet	duckling
hour	miniskirt	cup	key

Write 'there', 'their' or 'they're' in each gap. Don't forget capital letters if necessary.

> There, their and there are homophones. Homophones are words that have the same sound as another word but a different meaning or spelling.

25 _____ are my trainers, I wondered where they were!

26–27 _____ going to buy some with _____ money.

28 Is it _____ turn or mine?

29 Do you think _____ going to be late?

30 Do we need to go _____ tonight?

Now go to the Progress Chart to record your score! Total 30

Focus test 10 — Comprehension 2

The Great Mouse Plot

My four friends and I had come across a loose floor-board at the back of the classroom, and when we prised it up with a blade of a pocket-knife, we discovered a big hollow space underneath. This, we decided, would be our secret hiding place for sweets and other small treasures such as conkers and monkey-nuts and birds' eggs. Every afternoon, when the last lesson was over, the five of us would wait until the classroom had emptied, then we would lift up the floor-board and examine our secret hoard, perhaps adding to it or taking something away.

One day, when we lifted it up, we found a dead mouse lying among our treasures. It was an exciting discovery. Thwaites took it out by its tail and waved it in front of our faces. 'What shall we do with it?' he cried.

'It stinks!' someone shouted. 'Throw it out of the window quick!'

'Hold on a tick,' I said. 'Don't throw it away.'

Thwaites hesitated. They all looked at me.

When writing about oneself, one must strive to be truthful. Truth is more important than modesty. I must tell you, therefore, that it was I and I alone who had the idea for the great and daring Mouse Plot. We all have our moments of brilliance and glory, and this was mine.

'Why don't we,' I said, 'slip it into one of Mrs Pratchett's jars of sweets? Then when she puts her dirty hand in to grab a handful, she'll grab a stinky dead mouse instead.'

The other four stared at me in wonder. Then, as the sheer genius of the plot began to sink in, they all started grinning. They slapped me on the back. They cheered me and danced around the classroom. 'We'll do it today!' they cried. 'We'll do it on the way home! *You* had the idea,' they said to me, 'so *you* can be the one to put the mouse in the jar.'

Thwaites handed me the mouse. I put it into my trouser pocket. Then the five of us left the school, crossed the village green and headed for the sweet-shop. We were tremendously jazzed up. We felt like a gang of desperados setting out to rob a train or blow up the sheriff's office.

'Make sure you put it into a jar which is used often,' somebody said.

'I'm putting it in Gobstoppers,' I said. 'The Gobstopper jar is never behind the counter.'

'I've got a penny,' Thwaites said, 'so I'll ask for one Sherbert Sucker and one Bootlace. And while she turns away to get them, you slip the mouse in quickly with the Gobstoppers.'

Thus everything was arranged. We were strutting a little as we entered the shop. We were the victors now and Mrs Pratchett was the victim. She stood behind the counter, and her small malignant pig-eyes watched us suspiciously as we came forward.

'One Sherbet Sucker, please,' Thwaites said to her, holding out his penny.

I kept to the rear of the group, and when I saw Mrs Pratchett turn her head away for a couple of seconds to fish a Sherbert Sucker out of the box, I lifted the heavy glass lid of the Gobstopper jar and dropped the mouse in. Then I replaced the lid as silently as possible. My heart was thumping like mad and my hands had gone all sweaty.

'And one Bootlace, please,' I heard Thwaites saying. When I turned round, I saw Mrs Pratchett holding out the Bootlace in her filthy fingers.

'I don't want all the lot of you troopin' in 'ere if only one of you is buyin',' she screamed at us. 'Now beat it! Go on, get out!'

As soon as we were outside, we broke into a run. 'Did you do it?' they shouted at me.

'Of course I did!' I said.

'Well done you!' they cried. 'What a super show!'

I felt like a hero. I *was* a hero. It was marvellous to be so popular.

From *Boy*, Roald Dahl's autobiography

Answer these questions.

1 Where was the secret hiding place?

2 What was hidden in the secret hiding place?

3 Why do you think the friends were excited about finding a dead mouse?

4 Whose idea was it to do something with the mouse?

5 What is Roald Dahl suggesting when he says, 'We all have our moments of brilliance and glory, and this was mine'?

6 What do the friends plan to do with the mouse?

7 Does the passage suggest that the sweet shop is far from the school?

8–9 Describe how you think Roald Dahl felt as he approached the shop.

10 Was Roald Dahl successful in executing the plan?

11 Which line in the passage suggests how nervous Roald Dahl was?

12–13 The friends obviously don't like Mrs Pratchett very much. Find two pieces of evidence in the passage that support this.

14–15 How do you think Mrs Pratchett would have felt on discovering the mouse. Explain your answer.

Now go to the Progress Chart to record your score! Total 15

Focus test 11 — Spelling 3

Each of these words has a missing silent letter. Rewrite each word correctly.

1. sience _____
2. nome   _____
3. sissors _____
4. thum   _____
5. autum   _____
6. onest   _____

> Silent letters can be at the beginning, middle or end of the word.

Match these **prefixes** with their meanings.

> Think of a word with the prefix. This may help give you a clue to its meaning.

7	aqua	across
8	aero	against
9	trans	distance/from afar
10	micro	water
11	tele	air
12	anti	small

Write the **plural** form of each of these **nouns**.

> Remember, for most words ending in *f* or *fe*, you drop the *f* or *fe* and add *ves*.

13. thief _____
14. knife _____
15. calf _____
16. elf   _____
17. half _____
18. wife _____

Add the **suffixes** to these words ending in y.

> Don't forget any necessary spelling changes.

19 easy + ly   = _____
20 carry + er   = _____
21 journey + ing = _____
22 play + ful   = _____
23 busy + est   = _____
24 employ + ment = _____

Write each of these words correctly.

> Each word has a missing letter.

25 akward   _____
26 resturant   _____
27 defnite   _____
28 exagerate   _____
29 haras   _____
30 interupt   _____

Focus test 12 — Sentences 3

State whether each of these sentences has an **active** or **passive verb**.

> An active verb is when the main person or thing does the action.
> A passive verb is when the main person or thing has the action done to it.

1. Daniel kicked the ball. _____
2. Dad had a drink spilled over him. _____
3. Nazar swam six lengths of the pool. _____
4. Tisha was hit by the frisbee. _____
5. Inky, the dog, was given a bath. _____
6. Jane finished her homework. _____

Change the following sentences into **indirect speech**.

> Indirect speech states what has been said without using the exact words or (speech marks).

7. "It is time for tea," said Mum.
   _____

8. "When do the holidays start?" asked Joe.
   _____

9. "Do I have to clean out my rabbit?" Jacob queried.
   _____

10. "I am off to the park now," said Mia.
    _____

11. "I think the phone is ringing," stated Tom.
    _____

Add the missing semicolons to these sentences.

> Often semicolons separate two main clauses that are closely related to each other.

12. I have a spelling test tomorrow morning I can't come out to play tonight.

13 Tuhil loves riding on his skateboard his tricks on it are amazing.

14 Tayla was afraid of the dark she always slept with the light on.

15 London is a lively city there are many things to see and do.

16 Kyle likes chocolate Jay likes cake.

Rewrite each of the following, using only two words, one of which should have an apostrophe.

> An apostrophe shows when something belongs to someone or something. For example, whiskers belonging to a lion = lion's whiskers.

17 lead belonging to the dog

18 coat belonging to Callum

19 pen belonging to teacher

20 hats belonging to policemen

21 radio belonging to the painter

22 cakes belonging to the children

Rewrite this sentence, adding the missing punctuation and capital letters.

> Remember, always check through your work carefully.

23–30 are you awake Toby whispered it is time for our midnight feast

Focus test 13 — Grammar 3

Complete the table.

Comparative adjectives compare two nouns. Superlative adjectives are applied to the most extreme of more than two nouns. Note: not all words need a suffix added.

1–6

	Comparative adjectives	Superlative adjectives
tall		
tired		most tired
good	better	
attractive		

What parts of speech are each of these words?

Each of the following parts of speech will match with one word below.

common noun   proper noun   collective noun   abstract noun
adjective   verb   adverb   conjunction
preposition   pronoun

7 inside   _____
8 Kyle   _____
9 road   _____
10 so   _____
11 surely   _____
12 team   _____
13 they   _____
14 happiness   _____
15 think   _____
16 miserable   _____

Key words

The following list includes definitions of key words for this topic that are referred to throughout the book. You can use these when working through the answers to aid understanding.
The meaning of each key word is also given in a grey box on the page where the key word first appears.

abbreviation a shortened form of a word or words
abstract noun a word referring to something that can't be identified with any of your five senses, such as an emotion or an idea
active verb when an active verb is used, the main person or thing in the sentence does the action, for example: Dan threw the ball.
adjectival phrase a group of words that give more detail about a noun; it is comprised mostly of adjectives and does not include a main verb
adjective a word that describes a noun
adverb a word that provides information on place (for example, here), time (for example, soon), or manner (for example, quickly). Adverbs can also highlight the degree of possibility (for example, perhaps)
alphabetical order the order in which letters are found in the alphabet
antonym a word that has the opposite meaning to another word – for example, hot and cold are antonyms
clause a section of a sentence that includes a main verb
collective noun a word referring to a group, for example swarm, flock
common noun a word for general people, places or things
compound word a word made up of two other words, for example toothbrush
conjunction a word that connects two words, phrases or clauses, for example and, but
contraction a word that is a shortened version of two words, with an apostrophe placed where the letter(s) have been removed, for example do not = don't
definition the meaning of a word
diminutive a word implying smallness, for example booklet
formal (language) used when being respectful or when acting in an official capacity; it may include longer and more complex words
homophone a word that has the same sound as another word but a different meaning or spelling, for example write and right

indirect speech the reporting of what has been said without using the exact words or inverted commas (speech marks)
informal (language) used among friends or family, or with people you know well; it is often casual and relaxed, and may include shorter words and contractions
metaphor a figurative expression in which something is described in terms usually associated with another thing, for example: The sky is a sapphire sea.
modal verb a verb that changes the meaning of other verbs in a sentence, for example: You should tie your shoelaces. Some modal verbs suggest something is possible, for example: We may not get there in time.
noun a word for somebody or something
noun phrase a group of words describing a noun, for example: the big, red house. A noun phrase doesn't have a verb
object the person or thing which is affected by the action of a verb. For example, in the sentence 'Jack ate an ice cream', the object is 'ice cream'.
onomatopoeic an onomatopoeic word echoes a sound associated with its meaning, for example hiss
parenthesis a word or phrase that is separated off from the main sentence by brackets, commas or dashes, usually because it contains additional information not essential to understanding the sentence
passive verb when a passive verb is used, the main person or thing in the sentence has the action done to it, for example: The ball was thrown by Dan.
past tense the form of the verb that shows that something has happened
phrase a group of words that act as a unit but do not include a main verb
plural more than one
possessive pronoun a pronoun that shows to whom something belongs, for example mine, yours

prefix a group of letters added to the beginning of a word to change its meaning, for example un, dis
preposition a word that can give the position of something in relation to something else, for example on, above, behind
pronoun a word that takes the place of a noun
proper noun names of particular people, places, days of the week and so on. A proper noun begins with a capital letter
proverb a short saying that gives advice or tells you something
root word the word to which prefixes and suffixes are added to make another word
simile a figurative expression that describes something by comparing it with another thing, usually using the words 'like' or 'as', for example: as cold as ice

singular one
subject the person or thing who does the action expressed by the verb. For example, in the sentence 'Jack ate an ice cream', the subject is 'Jack'.
suffix a group of letters added to the end of a word to change its meaning
synonym a word with the same or similar meaning to another word, for example quick is a synonym of fast
verb a doing or being word

Focus test 1: Spelling 1 (pages 4–5)

1 a**tt**ached
2 co**mm**ittee
3 a**cc**ompany
4 reco**mm**end
5 progra**mm**e
6 co**rr**espond
7 i**s**land
8 **k**night
9 s**c**enery
10 desi**g**n
11 crum**b**
12 bu**d**get

13–18 Refer to definitions of plural and noun in key words on page A1.
13 **ladies**
14 **countries**
15 **toys**
16 **babies**
17 **trolleys**
18 **flies**

19–24 If the root word would take the suffix 'tion' in its noun form, use the suffix 'tious'.
19 **cious** suspicious The noun form is suspicion.
20 **tious** nutritious The noun form is nutrition.
21 **cious** malicious The noun form is malice.
22 **cious** vicious
23 **tious** fictitious The noun form is fiction.
24 **tious** ambitious The noun form is ambition.

25–30 Refer to definition of prefix in key words on page A2.
25 **un** unbroken
26 **im** impolite
27 **im** impure
28 **il** illegal
29 **un** unfounded
30 **il** illogical

Focus test 2: Sentences 1 (pages 6–7)

1–6 A command begins with an imperative verb and is an instruction for someone; it can end with an exclamation mark. A question requires an answer and ends with a question mark. A statement is a sentence that contains information and ends in a full stop.
1 **question**
2 **question**
3 **command**
4 **statement**
5 **statement**
6 **command**

7–13 Refer to definition of proper noun in key words on page A2.
As **E**mily ran towards **C**irencester **P**ark, she knew she was late. **S**he just hoped **A**rchie had waited for her. **H**e was going to swap his movie with her *Harry Potter* book but she knew he would be in a hurry.

14–18 Refer to definitions of clause and phrase in key words on page A1. Child's own sentences, e.g. *Mr Churchill kept an eye on the children in the pool as they dived in the deep end to retrieve their goggles.*

19–24 Refer to definition of past tense in key words on page A1. Answers in the simple past tense as given below are most likely, but other past tenses (for example 'was sleeping' or 'had slept') would also be acceptable.

19 slept
20 found
21 rode
22 went
23 made
24 poured
25–30 "When will tea be ready**?**" moaned Freddie. "I'm starving**!** It has to be soon**.**"

Focus test 3: Grammar 1 (pages 8–9)

1–6 Refer to definitions of proper noun, abstract noun and collective noun in key words on pages A1–A2. Possible answers include:
1–2 *Tim, India*
3–4 *love, hate*
5–6 *swarm, herd*
7–12 Refer to definitions of verb and noun in key words on pages A1–A2. Root words ending in 't' or 'te' usually take the suffix 'tion'; those ending in 'ss' or 'mit' take 'ssion'; 'sion' is used if the root word ends in 'd', 'de' or 'se'.
7 discuss
8 divide
9 alter
10 dictate
11 create
12 celebrate
13–18 Refer to definitions of adjectival phrase and noun in key words on page A1. Child's own answers.
19–24 Refer to definitions of conjunction, phrase and clause in key words on page A1. Possible answers include:
19 *and*
20 *as*
21 *because*
22 *so*
23 *but*
24 *although*
25–30 Refer to definition of preposition in key words on page A2.
25 towards
26 in
27 behind
28 inside
29 over
30 on

Focus test 4: Vocabulary 1 (pages 10–11)

1–6 Refer to definition of abbreviation in key words on page A1.
1 Dr
2 US
3 cm
4 Ltd
5 hr
6 GB
7–12 Refer to definition of alphabetical order in key words on page A1.
7 number
8 nun
9 nurse
10 nutmeg
11 nutty
12 nuzzle
13–17 Refer to definition of metaphor in key words on page A1. Child's own answers.
18–23 Refer to definition of root word in key words on page A2.
18 un**clean**
19 **agree**able
20 **destruct**ive
21 im**pure**
22 **inspect**ion
23 **plan**ning
24–30 Refer to definition of compound word in key words on page A1.
24 nightgown
25 armchair
26 bulldog
27 chopstick
28 daydream
29 keyhole
30 overdue

Focus test 5: Comprehension 1 (pages 12–13)

1 *in the backyard* (line 4)
2 *to the stars* (line 6)
3 *Monday* (line 9)
4 *Mars* (line 8)
5–6 *They had disappeared; Mrs Driver from next door was a witness* (lines 13–14).
7 *This suggests that the aliens knew what they wanted.*
8–9 *The aliens needed to block off a draught* (lines 23–24); *the aliens were collecting items from space for display in a museum* (lines 25–26).
10 *It states the underpants that went missing were 'Y-fronts', underpants that boys wear* (line 27).
11 *someone who lives on Earth*
12–13 *Yes – the second and fourth lines of each verse rhyme.*
14–15 Child's favourite verse and why they chose it, for example: *it was funny; it was a clever idea.*

Focus test 6: Spelling 2 (pages 14–15)

1. **necessary**
2. **embarrassed**
3. **sufficient**
4. **temperature**
5. **dictionary**
6. **opportunity**

7–12 If the adjective form of the word takes the 'ant' suffix, then 'ance' will be used for the noun form; if the adjective form takes the 'ent' suffix, then 'ence' will be used for the noun form.

7. **reference**
8. **obedience** The adjective form is obedient.
9. **extravagance** The adjective form is extravagant.
10. **licence**
11. **ignorance** The adjective form is ignorant.
12. **fragrance** The adjective form is fragrant.
13. gen<u>e</u>ral
14. secret<u>a</u>ry
15. int<u>e</u>rest
16. dictio<u>a</u>ry
17. ori<u>g</u>inal
18. fami<u>l</u>y

19–24 Although the general 'i before e except after c' rule can be applied sometimes, there are many exceptions. When the sound is ee, use 'ie' (e.g. bel<u>ie</u>f); when the sound is ay, use 'ei' (e.g. n<u>ei</u>ghbour). As usual, there are also some exceptions to this rule, such as caff<u>ei</u>ne.

19. rev<u>ie</u>w
20. v<u>ei</u>l
21. th<u>ei</u>r
22. f<u>ie</u>rce
23. f<u>ie</u>ry
24. c<u>ei</u>ling

25–30 Refer to definition of contraction in key words on page A1.

25. **they'll**
26. **I've**
27. **he'll**
28. **isn't**
29. **should've**
30. **there's**

Focus test 7: Sentences 2 (pages 16–17)

1–6 Refer to definitions of clause, phrase and parenthesis in key words on page A1.

1. To make ice cubes**,** pour cold water into the mould and put in the freezer.

2–3. The old lady**,** frail and unsteady**,** carried her shopping home.

4. Carys collected her certificate**,** medal and winning prize money from the major.

5–6. The mango**,** sweet and juicy**,** tasted delicious.

7. Kirkwood Secondary School specialises in two areas**:** sport and technology.

8. Our journey took us on many modes of transport**:** car, plane and train.

9. Aimee entered two classes in the local horse show**:** the jumping class and the fancy-dress class.

10. I want you to bring the following things to school tomorrow**:** a towel, your swimming costume and a change of clothes.

11. Tia loves many sports**:** netball, swimming, football and tennis.

12–17. "I can't wait for the performance," said Ellie. / "Nor can I!" replied Dan. / "Which scene are you in?" asked Tuhil. / "I'm in the first scene," said Dan. "I bet I feel very nervous the first time we do it." / "I know I will be terrified but I still can't wait," laughed Izzy. / "Shall we practise at playtime?" Ellie asked. / "Great idea!" they all responded.

18–30. Refer to grey box accompanying Focus test 2 Q7–13 for use of capital letters. Inverted commas (speech marks) should surround direct speech and always include punctuation.

18–22. "**P**lease can I take your dog for a walk**?**" asked **J**ulia.

23–30. "**I am so tired,**" said **S**imon**,** yawning**. "I am going to bed early tonight.**" Fulls stop after 'yawning' could be replaced by a comma.

Focus test 8: Grammar 2 (pages 18–19)

1–6 Refer to definitions of adjective and modal verb in key words on page A1. Child's own answer.

7–12 Refer to definition of pronoun in key words on page A2.
mine, his, you, they, theirs, I

13–18 Refer to definitions of adverb and verb in key words on pages A1–A2. Various answers are possible.

13. **speedily** or **carefully**
14. **soon**
15. **carefully** or **slowly** or **playfully**
16. **playfully** or **carefully**
17. **soon** or **perhaps**
18. **often** or **carefully** or **speedily**
19. <u>caught</u>, catch
20. <u>liked</u>, like
21. <u>were</u>, was
22. <u>ate</u>, eat
23. <u>write</u>, wrote
24. <u>find</u>, found

25–30 Refer to definitions of verb, adjective, adverb, noun and preposition in key words on pages A1–A2.

25. **going**
26. **cloudy**
27. **there**
28. **choir**
29. **beneath**
30. **ate**

Focus test 9: Vocabulary 2
(pages 20–21)

1–6 Refer to definition of synonym in key words on page A2. Possible answers include: *observe, glance, peer, inspect, look, stare*

7–10 Refer to definition of onomatopoeic in key words on page A2. Possible answers include:
7–8 *miaow, purr*
9–10 *beep, vroom*

11–14 Refer to definitions of formal and informal in key words on page A1.
11 **commence – start**
12 **request – ask for**
13 **terminate – end**
14 **endeavour – try**

15–18 Refer to definition of definition in key words on page A1. Possible answers include:
15 *unable to be seen*
16 *sleepy*
17 *not letting sound in or out*
18 *a decision of guilt or innocence; an opinion on something*

19–24 Refer to definition of diminutive in key words on page A1.
droplet, minibus, kitchenette, piglet, duckling, miniskirt

25–30 Refer to definition of homophone in key words on page A1. 'There' refers to a place; 'their' shows belonging to someone; 'they're' is a contraction of 'they are'.
25 **There**
26–27 **They're, their**
28 **their**
29 **they're**
30 **there**

Focus test 10: Comprehension 2
(pages 22–23)

1 *under a floorboard at the back of the classroom* (lines 1–3)
2 *sweets, conkers, monkey-nuts and birds' eggs (treasures)* (lines 3–4)
3 Child's own answer suggesting the friends were excited to see the dead mouse as it was something different and unexpected.
4 *Roald Dahl's* (lines 15–16)
5 *how amazing he is because he had such a wonderful idea* (though some children may detect irony in the sentence)
6 *place the dead mouse in a sweet jar to shock Mrs Pratchett* (lines 17–18)
7 *No, the description of how to get to the sweet shop suggest it's just across the village green.* (line 24)
8–9 *Roald Dahl felt excited and daring as he headed for the sweet shop, though he might also have felt nervous.* ('We were tremendously jazzed up', lines 24–25.)
10 *Yes* (lines 34–37)
11 *'My heart was thumping like mad and my hands had gone all sweaty.'* (line 37)
12–13 Answers may include: *they describe her in disrespectful terms, talking about her 'dirty hand' (line 18) and her 'small malignant pig-eyes' (line 32); they describe putting the mouse in a sweet jar (which will upset Mrs Pratchett and make the sweets unsaleable) as a 'super show'* (line 44).
14–15 Child's own answer.

Focus test 11: Spelling 3 (pages 24–25)

1 s**c**ience
2 **g**nome
3 s**c**issors
4 thum**b**
5 autum**n**
6 **h**onest

7–12 Refer to definition of prefix in key words on page A2.
7 **water**
8 **air**
9 **across**
10 **small**
11 **distance / from afar**
12 **against**

13–18 Refer to definitions of plural and noun in key words on page A1.
13 **thieves**
14 **knives**
15 **calves**
16 **elves**
17 **halves**
18 **wives**

19–24 Refer to definition of suffix in key words on page A2. If a word ends in a consonant and a 'y', the 'y' is often changed to an 'i' when adding a suffix.
19 **easily**
20 **carrier**
21 **journeying**
22 **playful**
23 **busiest**
24 **employment**
25 a**w**kward
26 rest**a**urant
27 de**fi**nite
28 exa**gg**erate
29 haras**s**
30 inter**r**upt

Focus test 12: Sentences 3
(pages 26–27)

1–6 Refer to definitions of active verb and passive verb in key words on page A1.
1 **active**   2 **passive**
3 **active**   4 **passive**
5 **passive**   6 **active**

7–11 Refer to definition of indirect speech in key words on page A1.
7 **Mum said that it was time for tea.** The word 'that' can be left out.
8 **Joe asked when the holidays started.**
9 **Jacob queried whether he had to clean out his rabbit.**
10 **Mia said that she was now off to the park.** The word 'that' can be left out.
11 **Tom stated that he thought the phone was ringing.** The word 'that' can be left out.

12–16 Refer to definition of clause in key words on page A1.
12 I have a spelling test tomorrow morning**;** I can't come out to play tonight.
13 Tuhil loves riding on his skateboard**;** his tricks on it are amazing.
14 Tayla was afraid of the dark**;** she always slept with a light on.
15 London is a lively city**;** there are many things to see and do.
16 Kyle likes chocolate**;** Jay likes cake.

17 **dog's lead**   18 **Callum's coat**
19 **teacher's pen**   20 **policemen's hats**
21 **painter's radio**   22 **children's cakes**

23–30 Refer to grey box accompanying Focus test 2 Q7–13 for use of capital letters. Inverted commas (speech marks) should surround direct speech and always include punctuation.

"**A**re you awake?" **T**oby whispered. "**I**t is time for our midnight feast**.**"

Focus test 13: Grammar 3
(pages 28–29)

1–6 Refer to definition of suffix in key words on page A2.

	Comparative adjectives	Superlative adjectives
tall	taller	tallest
tired	more tired	most tired
good	better	best
attractive	more attractive	most attractive

7–16 Refer to definitions of common noun, proper noun, collective noun, abstract noun, adjective, verb, adverb, conjunction, preposition and pronoun in key words on pages A1–A2.
7 **preposition**
8 **proper noun**
9 **common noun**
10 **conjunction**
11 **adverb**
12 **collective noun**
13 **pronoun**
14 **abstract noun**
15 **verb**
16 **adjective**

17–24 Refer to definitions of object, pronoun and subject in key words on pages A1–A2. Grammar questions will sometimes ask you to choose a personal pronoun to put in place of a name. In real life, the appropriate personal pronoun to use for someone will vary – some people might want she/her or he/him, others might prefer they/them, whereas some will favour other terms entirely. At the time of going to print there has been no definitive guidance on personal pronouns in the curriculum from the Department of Education or exam boards. If you do have questions in your 11+ test that asks for a personal pronoun for a proper noun, we would advise picking the most traditional choice – usually she/he or her/him.

17–18 The girl pushed **the bike**. subject pronoun: **She**
19–20 The children watched **the match**. subject pronoun: **They**
21–22 The old woman stroked **the dog**. subject pronoun: **She**
23–24 The boy ignored **his brother**. subject pronoun: **He**

25–30 Refer to definitions of possessive pronoun and preposition in key words on pages A1–A2. Note that possessive pronouns take the place of a noun, and should not be confused with possessive determiners (my, your, etc.) that are added to a noun. Possible answers include:
25–26 *sprint, saunter*
27–28 *mine, yours*
29–30 *behind, over*

Focus test 14: Vocabulary 3
(pages 30–31)

1–6 Refer to definitions of antonym and prefix in key words on pages A1–A2.
1 **disappear**   2 **undo**
3 **inaccurate**   4 **irrelevant**
5 **unfriendly**   6 **impolite**

7–12 Refer to definition of simile in key words on page A2. Child's own answers.
13–18 Refer to definition of proverb in key words on page A2.
13 **Better late than never.**
14 **A rolling stone gathers no moss.**
15 **You scratch my back and I'll scratch yours.**
16 **A penny saved is a penny gained.**
17 **Two heads are better than one.**
18 **Barking dogs seldom bite.**
19 The **one-way** street was closed because of an accident.
20 The **chocolate-covered** raisins were eaten quickly.
21 The children built their den in a **run-down** shed.
22 Watch out for the **man-eating** shark!
23 Do you like **strawberry-flavoured** yoghurt?
24 Surprisingly I prefer the **sugar-free** drink the most.
25–30 Child's own answer, for example: *pyjamas, boomerang, pizza, piano, café, spaghetti.*

Focus test 15: Comprehension 3 (pages 32–33)

1 *True* (line 7)
2 *Ten thousand* (line 6)
3 *a soft jingle from the horses' harness and the creaking of the gun carriages the horses were pulling* (lines 8–9)
4–6 'All of England was mourning the death of one man.' (line 3)
'all the people of London were out on the streets' (lines 3–4)
'Ten thousand soldiers marched in procession' (line 6)
7 *a flag* ('flown from the masthead', line 15)
8 *Yes* ('The Prince of Wales', line 23)
9 *in St Paul's Cathedral, London* (line 26)
10 *'Victory' is the name of Admiral Nelson's ship* (line 13)
11 *Sam's* (line 36) or *the perspective of one of the crew of Nelson's flagship HMS Victory* (line 13)
12–13 Child's own description of Will Wilmet. Possible answers include: *he was the bosun; he was one of the older men in the crew; he was upset at the funeral; he was a kind, thoughtful man.*
14–15 Child's own answer.

Mixed paper 1 (pages 34–38)

1 *25 years* (title)
2 *on the Village Green* (line 10), though some answers may also mention *the village's Saxon church* (line 16)
3–4 *strawberries are ripe and easily available; weather is most likely good*
5–6 *The local community wait at the tables* (lines 12–13); *tickets are available at the local Post Office or the village hall* (lines 23–24).
7 'THE WORKS' could include everything – strawberries, cream, ice cream and shortbread.
8–9 Child's own answer, for example: *plants and books.*
10 Child's own answer, taking into consideration the type of music playing.
11–12 Child's own answer, taking into consideration that food and a drink are also included in the ticket price.
13–14 *The poster makes reference to the ancient lime trees and the Saxon church* (lines 12 and 16)
15–16 Child's own answer, recognising that the weather at the weekend could dictate numbers attending. For example: *If wet, fewer people would attend and so income would be lower, and strawberries might be left over.*
17–18 Child's own answer. Ideas might include: *serving the strawberries under cover, for example in the church or under gazebos; selling off strawberries in punnets; moving Barry's Big Band to a different venue, for example the village hall.*
19–20 Child's own answer, for example: *more pictures, fewer words.*
21–25 Refer to definition of suffix in key words on page A2.
21 **solidify**
22 **apologise** If a word ends in a consonant and a 'y', the 'y' is often changed to an 'i' when adding a suffix.
23 **lighten**
24 **fossilise**
25 **intensify** When adding a suffix beginning with a vowel to a root word ending in 'e', the 'e' is usually removed.
26 ✓
27 ✗
28 ✓
29 ✓
30 ✗
31 u**nn**ecessary
32 o**cc**urrence
33 su**gg**est
34 inte**rr**upt
35 o**cc**upation
36–39 Refer to definitions of common noun, abstract noun, proper noun and collective noun in key words on pages A1–A2. Possible answers include:
36 *table*   37 *love*
38 *London*   39 *litter*

40–43 Possible answers include:
  40 *borough*
  41 *tough*
  42 *bought*
  43 *plough*
44–47 Refer to definitions of object, pronoun and subject in key words on pages A1–A2.
44–45 The girl loved **acting**. Subject pronoun: **She**
46–47 The man mended **his broken bike**. Subject pronoun: **He**
48–50 Refer to definitions of formal and informal in key words on page A1.
  48 **formal**
  49 **informal**
  50 **formal**
51–55 Refer to definition of simile in key words on page A2. Possible answers include:
  51 *as blind as a bat*
  52 *as brave as a lion*
  53 *as fresh as a daisy*
  54 *as hot as a chilli*
  55 *as quiet as a mouse*
56–60 Refer to definition of synonym in key words on page A2. Possible answers include: *enjoyable, excellent, great, skilled, kind,* etc.
61–65 Refer to definition of root word in key words on page A2.
  61 **entertain**ing
  62 **scare**d
  63 **thunder**ous
  64 **press**ure
  65 re**collect**
66–70 Refer to definitions of clause and conjunction in key words on page A1. Child's own answers.
71–75 The verb 'was' is used where the subject is a singular; 'were' is used where the subject is plural, or with the second person pronoun 'you'.
  71 **was**
  72 **Were**
  73 **were**
  74 **was**
  75 **were**
76–80 Commas are used to separate clauses, phrases or items in a list. They can also be used for parenthesis, around a piece of information that adds information but is not vital for the sentence to make sense.
  76 Can we have tomato ketchup**,** mushy peas**,** onion rings and chips with our fish?
77–78 We ran**,** puffing and panting**,** trying to catch up with our escaped dog.
  79 With a huge shove**,** the old door finally opened.
  80 Hannah was sad as her belongings**,** her bed and her bike were packed into the removal van.

Mixed paper 2 (pages 39–43)

1 *early evening, after dark* (line 1)
2–3 *'That smell of burnt leaves, the early dark' suggests that it is autumn* (line 5); *lines referring to the apples could also suggest autumn*
4–5 *in the park; there were three boys* (lines 7–8)
6 *the leaf canopies of the trees*
7 *apples*
8–9 Child's own answer describing how the boys felt, for example: *nervous, excited.*
10 *because they tasted good but were stolen*
11–12 *the little adventure and the smell of the apples* (line 24)
13 *The poem implies that John is dead, buried under apple trees* (lines 26–27)
14 *approximately 40 years* ('he's fifty years old', line 25, so would have been about ten when the events happened)
15–16 *because of the adventure the boys had in an orchard*
17–18 Refer to definition of metaphor in key words on page A1. Answers could include: *'Street lamps spilled pools of liquid gold'* (line 3) *'The breeze was spiced with garden fires'* (line 4)
19–20 Child's own answer, giving reasons for their thoughts.
21–25 Refer to definition of contraction in key words on page A1.
  21 **she's**
  22 **could've**
  23 **it'll**
  24 **wasn't**
  25 **they're**
26–30 Generally, 'cial' follows a vowel and 'tial' follows a consonant (e.g. facial, partial). Some of the answers are exceptions to this rule, but in these instances, root words can sometimes help.
  26 **confidential** This follows the general rule.
  27 **artificial** This follows the general rule.
  28 **financial** The root word is 'finan<u>c</u>e'.
  29 **commercial** The root word is 'commer<u>c</u>e'.
  30 **initial** This is a root word in itself.
31–35 Refer to definitions of plural and noun in key words on page A1.
  31 **elephants** Most singular words can be made plural by adding an 's'.
  32 **dishes** Words ending in 's', 'sh', 'ch', 'x', or 'z' can be made plural by adding 'es'.
  33 **wolves** Words ending in 'f' or 'fe' can be made plural by changing the suffix to 'ves'.
  34 **zoos** Refer to Q31.
  35 **lilies** Words ending in 'y' can be made plural by changing the 'y' to 'ies'.

36–40 Refer to definition of preposition in key words on page A2.
36 The keys were knocked **underneath** the sofa.
37 The smoke could be seen **on** the horizon.
38 Jane looked **through** the keyhole.
39 Dan became caught **behind** the wheelie bin!
40 The dog slipped **off** the rock face.
41–46 Refer to definitions of formal and informal in key words on page A1.
41 **could've – could have**
42 **go in – enter**
43 **fix – repair**
44 **thanks – thank you**
45 **what – pardon**
46 **find out – discover**
47 Robert and Sammy **is** going on holiday. **are**
48 Laughing **were** all they could do! **was**
49 Keita the dog **were** excited about her walk. **was**
50 Jacob **are** doing homework. **is**
51–55 Refer to definition of alphabetical order in key words on page A1.
51 **raspberry**
52 **rattle**
53 **raven**
54 **ravioli**
55 **razor**
56–60 Refer to definition of antonym in key words on page A1. Possible answers include:
56 *bright*
57 *young*
58 *pull*
59 *disprove*
60 *robust*
61–65 Refer to definition of definition in key words on page A1. Possible answers include:
61 *uncaring, thoughtless*
62 *a plant that grows in the sea*
63 *a section of something*
64 *a group of fish*
65 *a short phrase often used in advertising*
66–69 A command begins with an imperative verb and is an instruction for someone. A question requires an answer and ends with a question mark. A statement is a sentence that contains information and ends in a full stop.
66 **statement**
67 **command**
68 **question**
69 **command**
70–76 Refer to grey box accompanying Focus test 2 Q7–13 for use of capital letters. Inverted commas (speech marks) should surround direct speech and always include punctuation.
Niall peered over the railings**. "L**ook**! I** can see the sleeping tiger**."**

The following alternative is also acceptable:
Niall peered over the railings**.** "**L**ook **– I** can see the sleeping tiger**!"**
77–80 Refer to definitions of active verb and passive verb in key words on page A1.
77 **active**
78 **active**
79 **passive**
80 **active**

Mixed paper 3 (pages 44–49)

1 *yes* (lines 2–4)
2 *because it is designed to work on the animals that spiders prey on, not humans* (lines 4–6)
3 *no* (lines 10–11)
4 *the flesh around the bite rots and dies* (lines 11–12)
5–6 *medicines that work against the venom of specific spiders. Should someone be bitten by a dangerous spider, they have an increased chance of surviving.* (lines 16–19)
7–8 *when they feel trapped or threatened, for example when a spider is resting in a glove or a shoe which someone then puts on* (lines 22–25)
9 *because our primate ancestors used to live where spiders lived, on forest floors or up in trees* (lines 31–33)
10–11 *It is believed that our fear of spiders is partly inborn and comes from a time when even a bite that was harmless could stop our ancestors from hunting and finding the food they desperately needed.*
12 *in jungles and forests* (line 43)
13 *yes* (lines 5–6)
14 *spiders remove flies, mosquitos and other bothersome insects* (lines 44–45)
15–16 Child's own answer, including an explanation.
17–18 Child's own answer.
19–20 Child's own two questions.
21–25 Although the general 'i before e except after c' rule can be applied sometimes, there are many exceptions. When the sound is ee, use 'ie' (e.g. bel**ie**f); when the sound is ay, use 'ei' (e.g. n**ei**ghbour). As usual, there are also some exceptions to this rule, such as caff**ei**ne.
21 p**ie**r
22 conc**ei**t
23 n**ei**ther
24 fr**ie**nd
25 rev**ie**w
26–31 Refer to definition of prefix in key words on page A2. Possible answers include:
26–27 *autobiography, automatic*

28–29 *disappear, distrust*
30–31 *microphone, microscope*
32 **especially**
33 **bruise**
34 **controversy**
35 **nuisance**
36–39 Refer to definitions of preposition and noun phrase in key words on pages A1–A2. Child's own answers.
40–44 Refer to grey box accompanying Focus test 13 Q1–6 for comparative and superlative adjectives.

	Comparative adjectives	Superlative adjectives
wise	wiser	wisest
angry	angrier	angriest
thoughtful	more thoughtful	most thoughtful

45–50 Refer to definitions of verb, pronoun and adverb in key words on pages A1–A2. Possible answers include:
45–46 *speak, swim*
47–48 *yours, they*
49–50 *slowly, soon*
51–55 Refer to definition of abbreviation in key words on page A1.
51 **Mister**
52 **British Broadcasting Company**
53 **Great Britain**
54 **anonymous**
55 **adjective**
56–60 Refer to definition of root word in key words on page A2. As a general rule (although there are exceptions), if the root word looks like a whole word, the suffix will most likely be '-able'; if the root word does not look like a whole word, the suffix will most likely be '-ible'.
56 **considerable**
57 **reliable**
58 **horrible**
59 **adorable**
60 **forcible**
61–65 Refer to definition of proverb in key words on page A2.
61 *The first in line will be seen to first.*
62 *A friend that needs your help is a really good friend.*
63 *It is better to arrive late (or do something late) than not at all.*
64 *No matter what the situation, however bad, you can always find something good in it.*
65 *If you are careful with your money, you will be able to save.*
66–69 Refer to definition of parenthesis in key words on page A1. Children's own answers.

70–75 Refer to grey box accompanying Focus test 12 Q17–22 for possessive apostrophes. Apostrophes used to indicate possession come after the noun and are followed by the letter 's'. Apostrophes used to mark plural possession come after the plural noun, which often ends in 's'; in this case, the extra 's' that usually follows the apostrophe is not needed.
70 **the man's shoes**
71 **the children's marbles**
72 **the bridesmaid's flowers**
73 **the gardener's spade**
74 **Leah's earrings**
75 **the libraries' books**
76–80 Refer to definition of indirect speech in key words on page A1.
76 **Helen said she wished she could watch the end of the film.**
77 **Fred asked if they could dance.**
78 **Tom screamed that the zombies were coming.**
79 **Dad said that he thought there was an accident ahead.**
80 **Kate moaned that the park was closed.**

Mixed paper 4 (pages 50–55)

1 *for bait* (line 2)
2 *a strange moaning sound* (lines 5–6)
3 *It had just been born and was unaware of the dangers of man.*
4 *take it home for his child to keep as a pet* (line 16)
5–6 *placed it close to the water's edge because he could see the distress of the mother seal* (lines 18 and 24)
7 *a stretch where the water flows fast and deep on the high tide* (lines 29–30)
8 *loch* (line 16)
9 *four* (line 27)
10 *they had heard their father say that the cockles were better across the trink* (lines 30–31)
11 *They were probably arguing about whether they should cross the trink because they had been told it was dangerous.*
12 *Tam* (line 39)
13 *because they were so busy picking cockles* (line 35)
14–15 Child's own description.
16 *grey-cloaked; plump, friendly face; round brown eyes* (lines 44–46)
17–18 *In return for giving my child back to the sea, I will return your three children to the land.* (lines 54–57)
19–20 Child's own answer.

21–25 When adding a suffix to a root word ending in 'fer', if the second syllable of the root word is stressed, double the 'r'; if the first syllable of the root word is stressed, leave it as is.
  21 **preferable**
  22 **reference**
  23 **preferred**
  24 **deferring**
  25 **preference**
26–30 Refer to definition of singular in key words on page A2.
  26 **class** Words ending in 's', 'sh', 'ch', 'x', or 'z' can be made plural by adding 'es'.
  27 **hoof** Words ending in 'f' or 'fe' can be made plural by changing the suffix to 'ves'.
  28 **tragedy** Words ending in 'y' can be made plural by changing the 'y' to 'ies'.
  29 **scissors** This is the 'trick question' referred to, as the plural noun 'scissors' does not exist in the singular form: scissors are always plural (short for 'a pair of scissors'). However some children may know noun phrases which use the word 'scissor', e.g. 'scissor-kick', 'scissor action'.
  30 **scratch** Refer to Q26.
31–35 Refer to definition of contraction in key words on page A1.
  31 **we + have**
  32 **would + not**
  33 **we + would** or **we + had**
  34 **it + is** or **it + has**
  35 **she + will**
36–37 Refer to definitions of adjective and adverb in key words on page A1. Child's own answer.
38–41 Refer to grey box accompanying Focus test 7 Q7–11 for colons. Refer to grey box accompanying Focus test 12 Q12–16 for semicolons.
  38 Lola was embarrassed**;** she went bright red.
  39 Ben has three best friends**:** Ahmed, Taylor and Tom.
  40 I slipped and fell off the ledge**;** I now walk with a crutch.
  41 Meena goes to two weekly clubs**:** fencing on Friday and gym on Saturday.
  42 **pronoun**
  43 **adverb**
  44 **common noun**
  45 **preposition**
  46 **verb** or **common noun**
  47 **pronoun**
  48 **abstract noun**
  49 **adjective**
  50 **conjunction**
51–56 Refer to definition of compound word in key words on page A1. Possible answers include:
  51 *airport*
  52 *bedtime*
  53 *checkout*
  54 *downstairs*
  55 *eyelid*
  56 *fireworks*
57–61 Refer to definition of homophone in key words on page A1.
  57 **flee**
  58 **mist**
  59 **plain**
  60 **stares**
  61 **lessen**
62–65 Possible answers include: *friend, colleague, teacher, companion*
66–80 Inverted commas (speech marks) should surround direct speech and always include punctuation. Where commas are placed inside speech marks, below, exclamation marks would also be acceptable.
"Shall we meet at the park after school**?**" asked Jake.
"Great idea and I'll bring my skateboard**,**" said Mia.
"I'll let the others know**,**" Jake replied, wandering to his lesson.
"Bye**,**" Mia yelled after him.

NOTES

In each sentence, underline the **object** and write a **pronoun** for each **subject**.

> In a sentence, the subject is the person or thing who does the action expressed by the verb, while the object is the person or thing which is affected by the action of a verb. A pronoun is a word usually used to replace a noun.

17–18 The girl pushed the bike.   subject pronoun: _____

19–20 The children watched the match.   subject pronoun: _____

21–22 The old woman stroked the dog.   subject pronoun: _____

23–24 The boy ignored his brother.   subject pronoun: _____

Write two examples of each of the following.

> A powerful verb is a verb that adds more interest to your writing.
> A possessive pronoun is a pronoun that shows to whom something belongs.
> A preposition gives us the position of something in relation to another thing.

25–26 powerful verb   _____   _____

27–28 possessive pronoun   _____   _____

29–30 preposition   _____   _____

Now go to the Progress Chart to record your score!   Total   30

Focus test 14 — Vocabulary 3

Write an **antonym** for each of these words by adding a **prefix**.

An antonym is a word that has the opposite meaning to another word.

un   im   ir   in   dis

1 appear   _____
2 do   _____
3 accurate _____
4 relevant _____
5 friendly _____
6 polite   _____

Write a **simile** using the following subjects.

A simile is an expression that describes something, by comparing it with another thing, usually using the words 'like' or 'as' for example 'as cold as ice'.

7 sun   _____
8 car   _____
9 beetle   _____
10 diamond _____
11 pillow   _____
12 thunder _____

With a line, match the beginning of the **proverb** with its end.

> A proverb is a short saying that gives advice or tells you something.

13 Better late   is a penny gained.
14 A rolling stone   are better than one.
15 You scratch my back   seldom bite.
16 A penny saved   gathers no moss.
17 Two heads   than never.
18 Barking dogs   and I'll scratch yours.

6

Add the missing hyphen to each of these sentences to make their meaning clearer.

> Hyphens are used to connect words. A hyphen can be used to make the meaning of a sentence clear (less ambiguous).

19 The one way street was closed because of an accident.
20 The chocolate covered raisins were eaten quickly.
21 The children built their den in a run down shed.
22 Watch out for the man eating shark!
23 Do you like strawberry flavoured yogurt?
24 Surprisingly I prefer the sugar free drink the most.

6

Write six words that are used in English but originally came from another language.

> Think carefully about the words you choose.
> You could choose words from any country: perhaps from France, India, Australia or Italy.

25–30 _____ _____ _____

_____ _____ _____

6

Now go to the Progress Chart to record your score!   Total   30

Focus test 15 — Comprehension 3

Victory

The sound of the drums was like the beating of a great slow heart. Muffled drums, they were, with black cloth over them. Everything was muffled that day, even the grey, clouded sky. All of England was mourning the death of one man, and all the people of London were out on the streets leading to St Paul's, and all the air was filled with the slow beat of the drums and the unending slow march of thousands of feet.

Ten thousand soldiers marched in procession that day, before and behind us, in that long step they keep for funerals, with the hesitation in it that breaks your heart. Marines were marching too, and the cavalry regiments trotting their horses slow, with a soft jingle of harness, and artillery with horses pulling the creaking gun carriages. Every man of us wore black stockings, with black crepe in our hats, and black ribbons hung from the horses' heads. Over the beat of the drums, sometimes you would hear the wailing lament of a pipe band, like London weeping.

And there were we, forty-eight of us from the crew of his flagship HMS *Victory*, walking in pairs: forty-eight seamen and marines, with the senior men up front carrying our poor flag, the tattered white ensign that had flown from the masthead at the Battle of Trafalgar and been shot through and through. The men held it up sometimes to show it to the people lining the streets, and some said you could hear a rustle like the sound of the sea as hundreds and hundreds of men took off their hats in respect. Me, all I could hear was the drums, and the feet, and the boom of the minute guns.

Dozens of carriages creaked along behind us, drawn by more jingling horses, filled with noblemen and officers. Thirty-two admirals in full dress uniform there were at the Admiral's funeral, and a hundred captains. There never was a funeral like it, not even for a king. The Prince of Wales rode in his crested carriage just in front of the funeral car, a long gun carriage made to look like our *Victory*, with high brow and stern, and a canopy swaying above our Admiral's coffin.

With music and high words the funeral service lasted for hours, inside St Paul's Cathedral. A great blaze of candles hung from the huge domed roof. At the very end, when the coffin was to be lowered into the ground, we seamen had been told to fold our ensign in ceremony and lay it on the top. But when Will Wilmet, the bosun, and three of the older men took up that shredded white cloth, Will gave a kind of sob – and suddenly all the men were reaching for our sad flag and it came apart, and they stuffed pieces of it into their jackets. And the coffin went down into the crypt, under the stone floor, for ever.

He was a good man, Wilmet. He gave me a scrap of the flag for my own afterwards, outside the cathedral, when we were gathering to march back through the streets of London without our Admiral.

"Here, young Sam," he said. "Here's a bit for you. Keep it till you die, and have it buried with you. Your own little bit of Nelson."

From *Victory* by Susan Cooper

Answer the questions.

1 This passage describes a funeral. True or false?

2 How many soldiers marched in the procession?

3 What noises does the writer associate with the horses?

4–6 Find three pieces of evidence that suggest this was a funeral for an important man.

7 What is an ensign?

8 Did royalty attend the funeral?

9 Where was the funeral held?

10 How does the title of the story relate to this passage?

11 From whose perspective is this recount written?

12–13 Describe Will Wilmet in your own words.

14–15 Imagine that you were a Londoner on the streets watching the funeral go past. Describe how you and others around you felt.

Now go to the Progress Chart to record your score! Total 15

Mixed paper 1

Somerton Strawberry Fair – 25th Anniversary

Date: 7 and 8 July
Time: 10am–5pm
Come and enjoy the STRAWBERRIES!

- Strawberries and cream
- Strawberries and shortbread
- Strawberries and ice cream
- Just strawberries
- or…THE WORKS!

The Village Green becomes transformed as we welcome visitors from far and wide to taste the delights of an English Village Strawberry Fair. Relax under the cooling ancient lime trees while you are waited on by the local community.

Summer Market with stalls selling gifts, clothing, jewellery, honey, food and furniture.

Come and wander through the village's Saxon church where live music will be playing throughout the weekend. The live music includes piano recitals, flute duets, soprano singing. Something for everyone.

On Saturday evening, on the Village Green, we welcome Barry's Big Band. Put on your dancing shoes and for just £5 enjoy the sounds and sights of this top-class band. All the family are welcome, food and a drink provided at no extra cost.

Tickets available from Somerton Post Office or from Somerton Preschool at the village hall.

Answer these questions.

1 How many years has the Somerton Strawberry Fair been running?

2 Where is the Strawberry Fair held in Somerton?

3–4 Give two reasons why you think the Strawberry Fair is held in July.

5–6 Find two pieces of evidence that suggest the locals run the fair.

7 What do you think 'THE WORKS' includes?

8–9 List two other things that could be sold at the Summer Market.

10 Although the poster states that everyone is welcome to the evening entertainment, what groups of people do you think will most enjoy it?

11–12 Do you think that the evening entertainment is good value for money? Why?

13–14 What evidence is there that Somerton is an old, well-established village?

15–16 How could the weather affect the success of the weekend?

17–18 What could the organisers do to overcome the problems of a very wet weekend?

19–20 How could this poster be improved?

_____

_____

Add the **suffix** *en*, *ify* or *ise* to each of these to make a word. Don't forget any necessary spelling changes.

21 solid   _____

22 apology   _____

23 light   _____

24 fossil   _____

25 intense   _____

Put a tick by the words spelt correctly and put a cross by those spelt incorrectly.

26 neighbour ☐

27 pesuade   ☐

28 sincere   ☐

29 vegetable ☐

30 desparate ☐

Add the correct double letters to complete each word.

31 u __ __ ecessary   32 o __ __ urrence

33 su __ __ est   34 inte __ __ upt

35 o __ __ upation

Write an example of each of the following.

36 common noun   _____

37 abstract noun   _____

38 proper noun   _____

39 collective noun _____

Write a word that rhymes with each of these *ough* words.

40 thorough _____   41 enough _____

42 fought _____   43 bough _____

In each sentence, underline the **object** and write a **pronoun** for each **subject**.

44–45 The girl loved acting.   subject pronoun: _____

46–47 The man mended his broken bike.   subject pronoun: _____

Do these sentences use **formal** or **informal** language?

48 Once they arrive, we will commence with the proceedings. _____

49 She's got a new bike, hasn't she? _____

50 Your quick response is appreciated. _____

Finish these **similes**, using your own words.

51 as blind as _____

52 as brave as _____

53 as fresh as _____

54 as hot as _____

55 as quiet as _____

Write five **synonyms** for the word 'good'.

56–60 _____   _____   _____

_____   _____

Underline the **root words** in each of these words.

61 entertaining   62 scared

63 thunderous   64 pressure

65 recollect

Add a **clause** with a **conjunction** to each of these main clauses.

66 The thunderstorm was frightening _____

_____

67 Jake fell off the swing _____

_____

68 The children on the rollercoaster screamed _____

_____

69 Dee slipped on the ice _____

_____

70 The teacher spoke quietly to her class _____

_____

Add 'was' or 'were' in each gap to make the sentences correct.

71 Meg _____ late for school.

72 _____ we on time for the football?

73 The children _____ soaking their dad with a hose.

74 The giant _____ terrifying.

75 Veejay and Tuhil _____ going to the dentist on Monday.

Add the missing commas to these sentences.

76 Can we have tomato ketchup mushy peas onion rings and chips with our fish?

77–78 We ran puffing and panting trying to catch up with our escaped dog.

79 With a huge shove the old door finally opened.

80 Hannah was sad as her belongings her bed and her bike were packed into the removal van.

Now go to the Progress Chart to record your score! Total / 80

Mixed paper 2

The Apple-Raid

Darkness came early, though not yet cold;
Stars were strung on the telegraph wires;
Street lamps spilled pools of liquid gold;
The breeze was spiced with garden fires.

That smell of burnt leaves, the early dark, 5
Can still excite me but not as it did
So long ago when we met in the park –
Myself, John Peters and David Kidd.

We moved out of town to the district where
The lucky and wealthy had their homes 10
With garages, gardens, and apples to spare
Ripely clustered in the trees' green domes.

We chose the place we meant to plunder
And climbed the wall and dropped down to
The secret dark. Apples crunched under 15
Our feet as we moved through the grass and dew.

The clusters on the lower boughs of the tree
Were easy to reach. We stored the fruit
In pockets and jerseys until all three
Boys were heavy with their tasty loot. 20

Safe on the other side of the wall
We moved back to town and munched as we went.
I wonder if David remembers at all
That little adventure, the apples' fresh scent.

Strange to think that he's fifty years old, 25
That tough little boy with scabs on his knees;
Stranger to think that John Peters lies cold
In an orchard in France beneath apple trees.

Vernon Scannell

Answer these questions.

1 At what time of day did the boys meet?

2–3 In which season is the poem based? Use a line from the poem to support your answer.

4–5 Where did the boys meet and how many were there?

6 What are 'the trees' green domes' (line 12)?

7 Verse 5 mentions the 'clusters'. What are in the clusters?

8–9 In your own words, describe how the boys felt having climbed the wall into the 'secret dark'.

10 Why were the apples described as the boys' 'tasty loot' (line 20)?

11–12 The poet wonders whether David remembers two things. What two things does he refer to?

13 Why does the poet just wonder what David remembers, rather than David and John?

14 Approximately how many years after the event is this poem written?

15–16 Why is it significant that John Peters lies in a French orchard, beneath apple trees?

17–18 What are two **metaphors** found in this poem?

_____

_____

19–20 How does this poem make you feel? What do you like or dislike about it?

_____

_____

_____

_____

Write the **contraction** for each of these.

21 she + has   = _____

22 could + have = _____

23 it + will   = _____

24 was + not   = _____

25 they + are   = _____

Add *cial* or *tial* to each of these to make a word.

26 confiden_____

27 artifi_____

28 finan_____

29 commer_____

30 ini_____

Write the **plural** form of each of these **nouns**.

31 elephant   _____

32 dish   _____

33 wolf   _____

34 zoo   _____

35 lily   _____

Underline the **preposition** in each sentence.

36 The keys were knocked underneath the sofa.

37 The smoke could be seen on the horizon.

38 Jane looked through the keyhole.

39 Dan became caught behind the wheelie bin!

40 The dog slipped off the rock face.

Match, with a line, the **informal** words with the **formal** options.

41 could've   pardon

42 go in   repair

43 fix   discover

44 thanks   could have

45 what   thank you

46 find out   enter

In each of these sentences a word is incorrect. Underline the word and rewrite it correctly.

47 Robert and Sammy is going on holiday.   _____

48 Laughing were all they could do!   _____

49 Keita the dog were excited about her walk. _____

50 Jacob are doing homework.   _____

Put these words in **alphabetical order**.

raven   razor   rattle   raspberry   ravioli

51 _____   52 _____

53 _____   54 _____

55 _____

Write an **antonym** for each of these words.

56 dull   _____   57 elderly   _____

58 shove   _____   59 prove   _____

60 delicate _____

Write a **definition** for each of these words.

61 selfish

62 seaweed

63 segment

64 shoal

65 slogan

What are the following: commands, questions or statements?

66 I would like to make some cakes _____

67 Be quick _____

68 Can you feed the dog _____

69 Stop screaming _____

Rewrite this sentence, adding the missing punctuation and capital letters.

70–76 niall peered over the railings look i can see the sleeping tiger

State whether each of these sentences has an **active** or **passive verb**.

77 Gina swung on the swing. _____

78 Tim watched the television. _____

79 Ivy was having her hair cut. _____

80 Oscar screamed loudly. _____

Mixed paper 3

Do we need to be scared by spiders?

There are over 40,000 known species of spider, yet fewer than 30 have venom that can cause serious illness in humans, and only a few (including Black and Brown Widow spiders, Funnel-web spiders and Brazilian Wandering spiders) are capable of killing with a bite. This is because spider venom typically only works on the animals (usually insects, but sometimes birds and small mammals) that the spider preys on. So most venomous spider bites cause, at worst, minor illness in humans and other animals not part of the spider's diet.

In fact, most of the spiders people think are 'deadly' aren't even dangerous. A bite from a Tarantula, for example, is very painful but certainly won't kill you. A bite from a Brown Recluse spider may look nasty, as it causes the flesh around it to rot and die, but there hasn't been a single confirmed death from one of those either.

Even Black Widows, which do have the ability to kill us, hardly ever succeed in doing so, because they rarely inject more than a tiny amount of venom per bite. Add to that the powerful antivenins (medicines which work against the venom of specific spiders) that are kept in hospitals to treat Black Widow bites, and the result is that the death rate has fallen to just one or two people per year, worldwide.

Most spiders are not aggressive, and prefer not to get close enough to humans to bite them. In fact, most spiders are even less keen on biting than snakes, and only bite if picked up, prodded or squashed. No venomous spider will charge or jump at you to bite, like they do in horror movies. Almost all spider bites happen when people put on gloves, footwear or other clothing in which the spider was resting. And think about it – if you were stuck in the toe of a giant boot, and a huge fleshy foot came down to squash you, what would you do? Everything you could to stop it, I should think. And that's all poor Spidey does.

The lowdown

Spiders, basically, get a bad rap. Our fear of them is deep, because it goes way, way back – perhaps to the time when our primate ancestors used to sleep on forest floors or up in trees, where they encountered spiders more often.

At least part of our fear of them seems to be inborn. This is possibly because that very fear helped our ancestors to survive. While spider bites rarely kill modern humans, it would have been a different story for our animal ancestors. One painful, swollen bite to the hand or foot could have stopped them from hunting. That would have made even non-lethal spider bites deadly in the long run.

But when you look at it, we really don't need these fears any more. Hardly any spiders pose a threat to us now, and they're generally easy enough to avoid, since we no longer have to go rooting around in the jungles and forests where most of the venomous ones live. If we can tolerate having spiders around, they actually do us a favour by removing mosquitoes, flies and other bothersome insects as part of their daily diet.

From *Stuff that scares your pants off!* by Glen Murphy

Answer these questions.

1 Are any spiders capable of killing a human?

2 Why is a spider's venom usually harmless to humans?

3 Is a Tarantula deadly?

4 What effect does a bite from a Brown Recluse spider have?

5–6 What are antivenins? What difference have they made?

7–8 When are spiders most likely to bite? Give examples.

9 Why would our primate ancestors have encountered spiders more often than we do now?

10–11 In your own words, explain where our fear of spiders might come from.

12 Where do most venomous spiders live?

_____

13 Can some spiders catch birds to eat?

_____

14 How do spiders help us?

_____

15–16 The passage states in line 40 that we no longer need to fear spiders. Do you agree? Why?

_____

_____

_____

17–18 Explain how this passage has changed how you might now react to spiders.

_____

_____

_____

19–20 Write two further questions you would like to ask about spiders that you can't find answers for in this passage.

_____

_____

Add *ie* or *ei* to each of these to make a word.

21 p __ __ r   **22** conc __ __ t

23 n __ __ ther   **24** fr __ __ nd

25 rev __ __ w

Write two words that begin with each of these **prefixes**.

26–27 auto   _____   _____

28–29 dis   _____   _____

30–31 micro   _____   _____

Circle the word that is spelt correctly.

32 espcially   especially

33 briuse   bruise

34 controversy   controvursy

35 nuisence   nuisance

Write two sentences, each with a **preposition** and a **noun phrase**.

36–37 _____

_____

38–39 _____

_____

Complete the table.

40–44

	Comparative adjectives	**Superlative adjectives**
wise	wiser	
angry		
thoughtful		

Write two examples of each of the following.

45–46 verb   _____   _____

47–48 pronoun   _____   _____

49–50 adverb   _____   _____

Write the following **abbreviations** in full.

51 Mr   _____

52 BBC   _____

53 GB   _____

54 anon.   _____

55 adj.   _____

47

Add *able* or *ible* to each of these **root words** to make a new word.

56 consider _____

57 rely _____

58 horror _____

59 adore _____

60 force _____

Write the meaning of each of these **proverbs**.

61 First come, first served.
_____

62 A friend in need is a friend indeed.
_____

63 Better late than never.
_____

64 Every cloud has a silver lining.
_____

65 A penny saved is a penny gained.
_____

Write two sentences. Each sentence needs to have two commas illustrating **parenthesis**.

66–67 _____
_____

68–69 _____
_____

Rewrite each of the following, using only two or three words, one of which should have an apostrophe.

70 shoes belonging to the man _____

71 marbles belonging to the children _____

72 flowers belonging to the bridesmaid _____

73 spade belonging to the gardener _____

74 earrings belonging to Leah _____

75 books belonging to the libraries _____

Write these sentences as **indirect speech**.

76 "I wish I could watch the end of the film," said Helen.

_____

77 "Can we dance?" asked Fred.

_____

78 "The zombies are coming!" screamed Tom.

_____

79 "I think there is an accident ahead," said Dad.

_____

80 "The park is closed," moaned Kate.

_____

Mixed paper 4

One Spared to the Sea

It is many years now since Willie Westness of Over-the-Watter was digging lugworms for bait in the little sandy bay on the east side of Elsness. By the time his pail was full, the tide had not yet turned. The trink was still safe to cross, and he decided to look for driftwood farther along the shore. Then it was that he heard the cry from the rocks – a moan like that of a woman in pain swelling into a loud, strange sound and dying into a sort of sob. It seemed to come from the geo, a little inlet hidden behind the rocks and covered at high tide. Out in the deep water a big seal had raised its head and was listening and watching intently.

Willie moved quietly towards the geo. Coming around the rocks that had hidden it, he saw, lying on the shelving stone, another big seal. Beside her was a newborn pup. As the mother began to move, he ran down over the rocks. The seal flopped into the water, but the pup lay helpless at his feet. It squirmed as he picked it up, and then pressed against him and nuzzled at his hand.

I'll take it home for the bairn, thought Willie, and keep it in the small loch at Over-the-Watter.

At the edge of the rocks the mother seal splashed and sobbed in distress. When he glanced up, she was pulling herself clumsily back out of the water to lie moaning at the edge, her round eyes full of tears. The pup too gazed at him with soft blurred brown eyes, and nosed at his sleeve. Its little sleek round head was like a child's ...

'Ach, selkie, take thee bairn and be gone wi' ye!' said Willie Westness aloud. He put the pup down close to the water's edge and watched the seal come to it. Then he collected his pail of lugworms and trudged back over the trink where the tide was just beginning to run.

Nine years afterwards, Willie Westness had a family of four. One fine day the three youngest went wading for cockles at the little sandy bay. They knew well enough that they should not cross the trink, where the water swept so fast and deep on the high tide. But they had heard their father say that the cockles were better there than in the large bay itself, and after a little argument among themselves, they crossed over.

"We won't stay long," said Johnny, the eldest.

"We'll hurry back," agreed his sister, Jeanie.

The cockles were plentiful, and they went on gathering. When the pail was nearly full, they turned towards home. The tide was flowing fast. The trink had widened.

"Hurry!" said Johnny.

But for all that he and Jeanie pulled and scolded, little Tam's fat legs could not be hurried over the rocks. Every minute the water deepened.

The two younger began to cry … but no one appeared across the trink to help them and the water rose steadily.

Then they heard a soft voice singing almost beside them. Two people had come up behind them – two grey-cloaked women that they did not know.

"Come away, bairns," said the elder. She had a plump, friendly face and round brown eyes. "Come away. It will soon be too late."

She took little Tam and Jeanie by the hands and led them straight into the water that was now up to their knees where they stood. Up to their middles it rose, and before they had crossed the trink, up to their necks. But held in her firm, warm grasp they kept their footing and found themselves in safety on the far side. Looking back, they saw their brother coming hand-in-hand with the smaller, slimmer woman.

"All's well," said the older woman cheerfully.

"Now take thee father a word from me," said the elder. "Remember now, to say to thee father, Willie Westness, to mind a day when he digged lugworm at the geo, nine summers gone. And say to him that one spared to the sea is three spared to the land."

And she gave them a little push. Obediently they ran. And when they looked back no grey-cloaked women were in sight, and two seals were swimming towards the point of Elsness.

Nancy and W. Towrie Cutt

Answer these questions.

1. Why was Willie digging for lugworms?

2. What alerted Willie to the seals?

3. Why do you think the seal pup did not move when Willie ran up to it?

4. What did Willie plan to do with the seal?

5–6. What did Willie do with the pup and why?

7. In your own words describe a 'trink' (line 3).

8 This story is based in Scotland. Find a word after the second paragraph that supports this statement.

9 Nine years later, how many children did Willie have?

10 Why did the children want to cross the trink?

11 What do you think the children were arguing about in line 32?

12 What was the name of Willie's youngest child?

13 Why did the children not notice the tide coming in until it was too late?

14–15 In your own words, describe the women that appeared.

16 What **adjectives** are used to describe the women that could also be used to describe the seals? List your answers.

17–18 What did the message sent to Willie by the elder woman mean?

19–20 Were you surprised by the ending of the story? How did it make you feel?

Complete these word sums. Don't forget any spelling changes.

21 prefer + able   = _____
22 refer + ence   = _____
23 prefer + ed   = _____
24 defer + ing   = _____
25 prefer + ence   = _____

Write the **singular** form of each word. Watch out, there is a trick question!

26 classes   _____
27 hooves   _____
28 tragedies   _____
29 scissors   _____
30 scratches   _____

Write the two words each **contraction** stands for.

31 we've   = _____ + _____
32 wouldn't = _____ + _____
33 we'd   = _____ + _____
34 it's   = _____ + _____
35 she'll   = _____ + _____

Write a sentence which includes an **adjective** and an **adverb**.

36–37 _____

Add the missing colon or semicolon to these sentences.

38 Lola was embarrassed she went bright red.
39 Ben has three best friends Ahmed, Taylor and Tom.
40 I slipped and fell off the ledge I now walk with a crutch.
41 Meena goes to two weekly clubs fencing on Friday and gym on Saturday.

What parts of speech are each of these words?

42 they _____

43 silently _____

44 camel _____

45 into _____

46 play _____

47 we _____

48 failure _____

49 rare _____

50 because _____

Add to each of these words to make a **compound word**.

51 air _____

52 bed _____

53 check _____

54 down _____

55 eye _____

56 fire _____

Write a **homophone** for each of these words.

57 flea _____

58 missed _____

59 plane _____

60 stairs _____

61 lesson _____

Write four nouns that can be used for both males and females.

62–65 _____   _____

_____   _____

Punctuate this passage correctly. Remember to start a new line when it is needed.

66–80 Shall we meet at the park after school asked Jake Great idea and I'll bring my skateboard said Mia I'll let the others know Jake replied wandering to his lesson Bye Mia yelled after him